When Kayla Was Kyle

Written by
Amy Fabrikant

Illustrated by
Jennifer Levine

The author warrants and represents that she has the legal right to publish or owns all material in this book. If you find a discrepancy, contact the publisher at www.avidreaderspg.com.

When Kayla was Kyle

Avid Readers Publishing Group

http://www.avidreaderspg.com

ISBN-13: 978-1-61286-154-8

Printed in the United States

I want to thank C.K. for sharing her story. She is one of the bravest people I know.

-ABFE

Let the first act of every morning
be a thought:
I shall not bear ill will toward
anyone.
Let the sun
climb high in the sky, and shed
its grace on every living thing.
It could happen.

“Don’t give up Kyle,” his dad said. “If it’s important, it’s worth fighting for.”

Kyle’s feet felt heavy in his sneakers, but determined to make his father proud, he kept shooting into the hoop.

“That’s the way, buddy!” Kyle’s dad cheered.

“I think I’m done for the night, dad,” Kyle said, rubbing his hands together for warmth.

“You did a great job tonight. Keep it up.”

Monday morning at school took away all of Kyle's confidence. He didn't have a partner for writing time and had to work with his teacher. At the end of writing workshop, Kyle's teacher shared his poem. Kyle could feel his cheeks turning red.

Kyle

In my dream
I plant a garden
of bright pink tulips
my Moms favorite flower
on a mountain
by a lake
I fly a plane
in a sky
without clouds
to a place where
no one laughs at
me
where everybody
plays together.

During free time in class, the boys ran to the trucks and the girls ran to the dollhouse.

Kyle thought about his father's words, "The boys won't like you if you do girl stuff."

Kyle sat outside of the boy's circle while the boys went….

CRASH!

BAM! BAM!

RRRRMMM! RRRRMMM!

EEEEEEK!

Kyle didn't make a sound.

While playing tag the bases in gym class, some boys laughed,

“Ha, ha, get that loser, Kyle out!”

Kyle didn’t try to get on base. He got tagged right away.

His head felt like it might explode tears that would flood the whole gym.

All Kyle wanted was to get home.

When Kyle's mom tucked him into bed that night, Kyle asked,

"Mom, do you think Dad will be really upset if I quit basketball?"

"Hmmmm…I think he might be a little disappointed. Why? What's the matter?" Kyle's mother asked.

"I just don't like the kids on the team that much, and they don't like me," Kyle answered.

"I don't think that's a good reason to quit. Quitting is never good. Let's talk to dad about it tomorrow. Okay Sweetie Pie?"

Kyle looked out his window at the stars.

"Kyle, are you listening?" His mother asked.

Kyle nodded yes, but his mind was on the stars. The stars were thousands of miles away, but everyone could see them. He wished he were a bright star.

"Don't worry," Kyle's mother told him. "It will all work out. Things always do."

"I love you, mommy," Kyle said.

"I love you, a whole bunch." Kyle's mother hugged him good night.

It was the night of the basketball game. Kyle didn't have that talk with his dad…he had a stomachache instead and stayed home.

The next week, Kyle hid his team jersey under his dress up clothes, but his father found it and insisted he go to the game. Kyle sat at the end of the bench the entire game.

Day after day, no matter how hard Kyle tried, the boys didn't include him. Many days, Kyle ended up at the author's table alone.

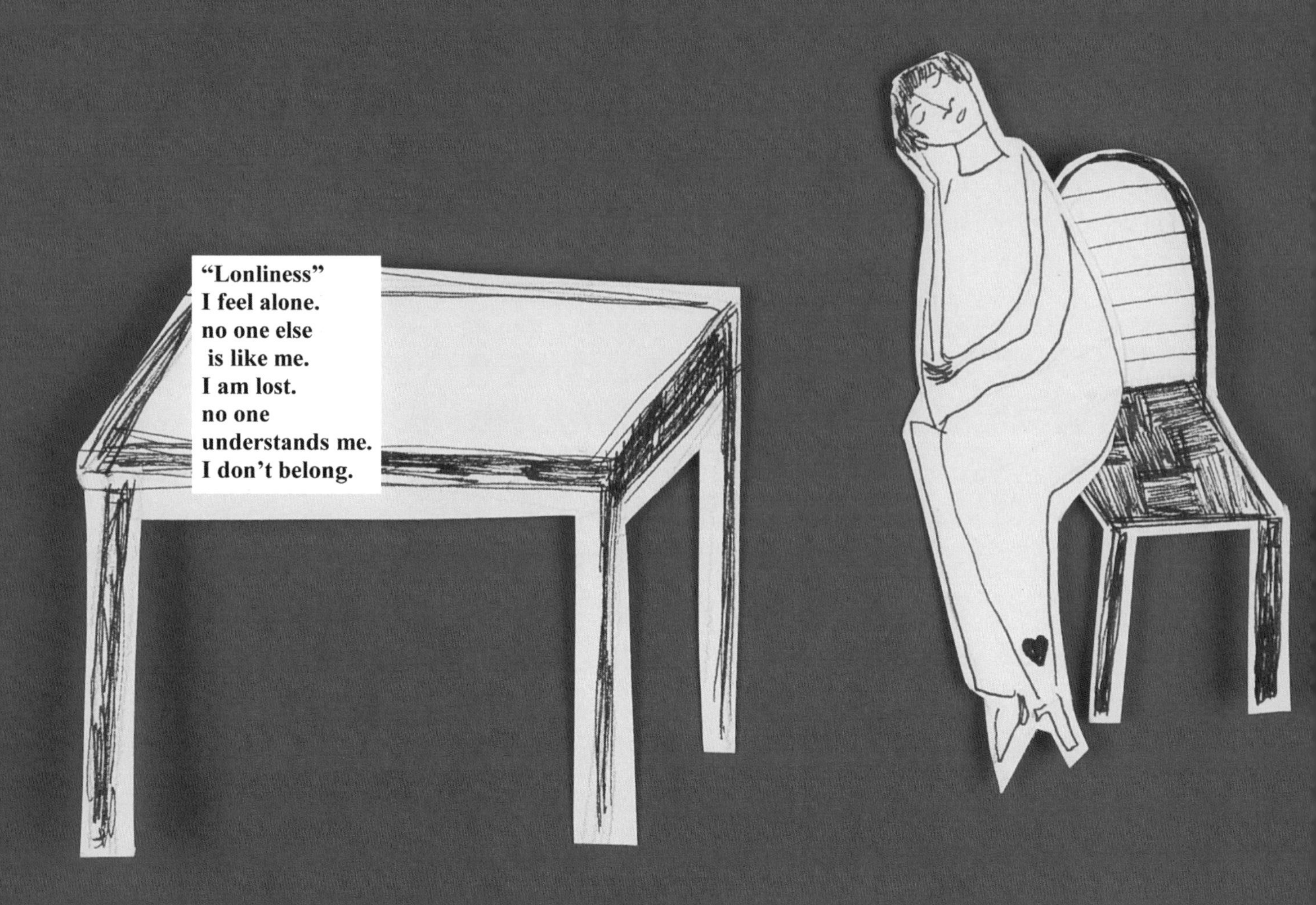

In bed at night, Kyle told his dad that he didn't want to play basketball anymore.

"I hardly play in the games and when I do, the boys don't pass to me." Kyle explained.

"I want to quit the team, Dad."

"You just need to hang in there, buddy." His dad said.

Kyle sighed.

"Make some plans with boys from your class. Shoot some hoops."

Kyle's dad said with a smile.

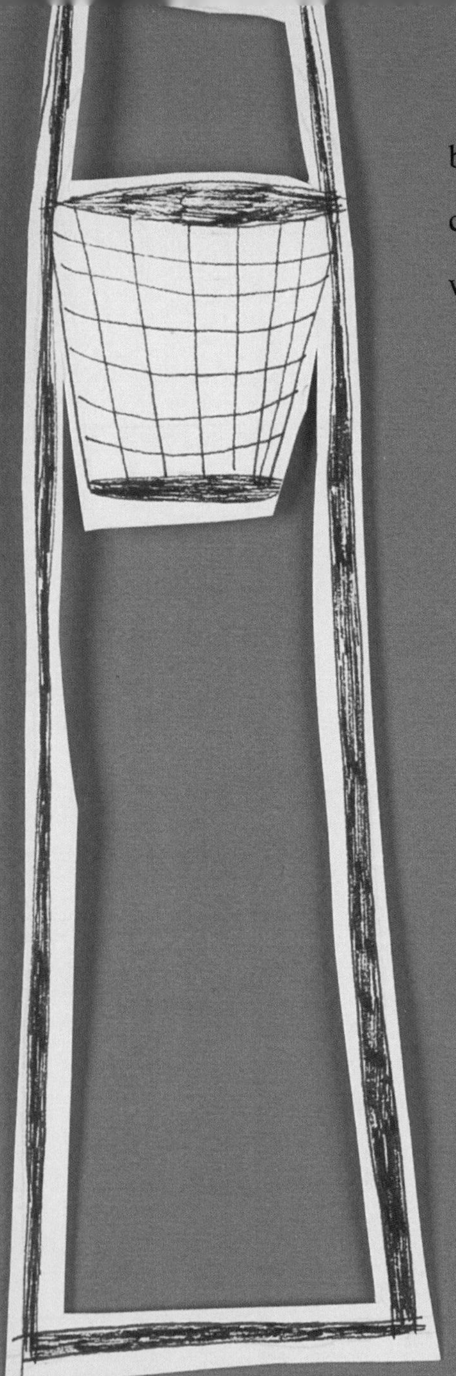

The next day, Kyle's mother arranged a playdate with a boy from his basketball team. Kyle and his friend shot hoops in the driveway, ate warm chocolate chip cookies, and played video games. Kyle asked, "What do you want to do now?"

"I don't know. What do you want to do?" replied Kyle's friend.

"Promise you won't tell anyone?" asked Kyle.

Kyle's friend nodded yes, and Kyle led him upstairs.

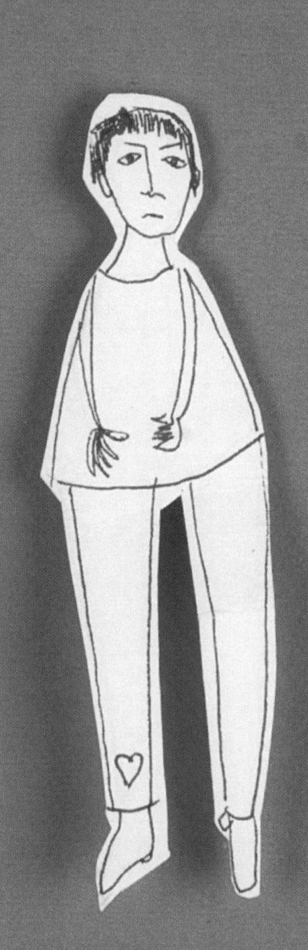

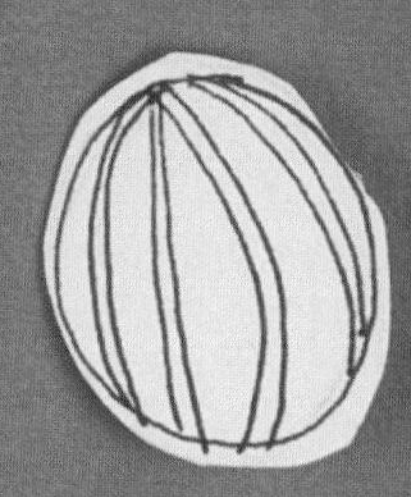

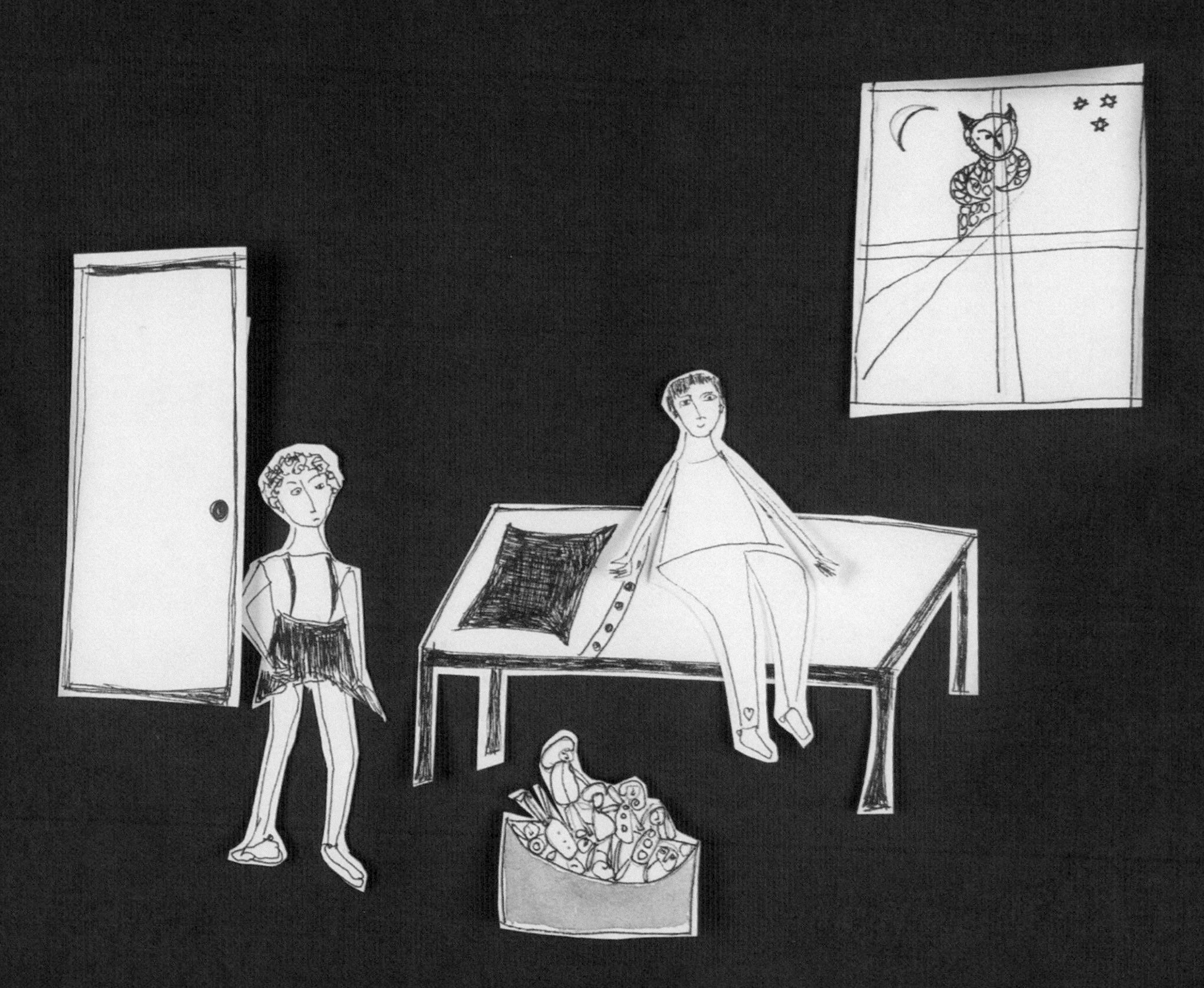

Kyle pulled out a box of Barbie dolls from under his bed and waited for the boy to laugh, but the boy shrugged. “That’s okay.”

Kyle felt so happy. He thought maybe he was wrong about the boys in his class. Maybe they could be friends.

But at school the next day…

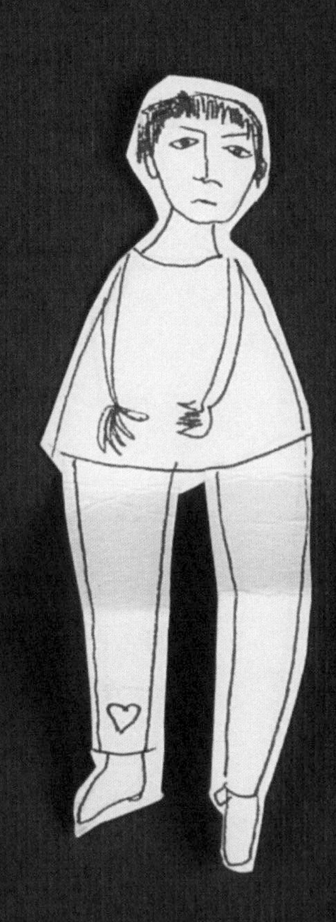

The kids teased Kyle.

“Kyle plays with dolls.

Kyle plays with dolls.”

Some boys whispered “Girl,” to Kyle.

No one talked to Kyle at lunch or played with him on the playground.

Kyle pretended to fit in at school. He became the class clown and got into trouble with his teachers, just to make the boys laugh, but he still couldn't find a seat at the lunch table.

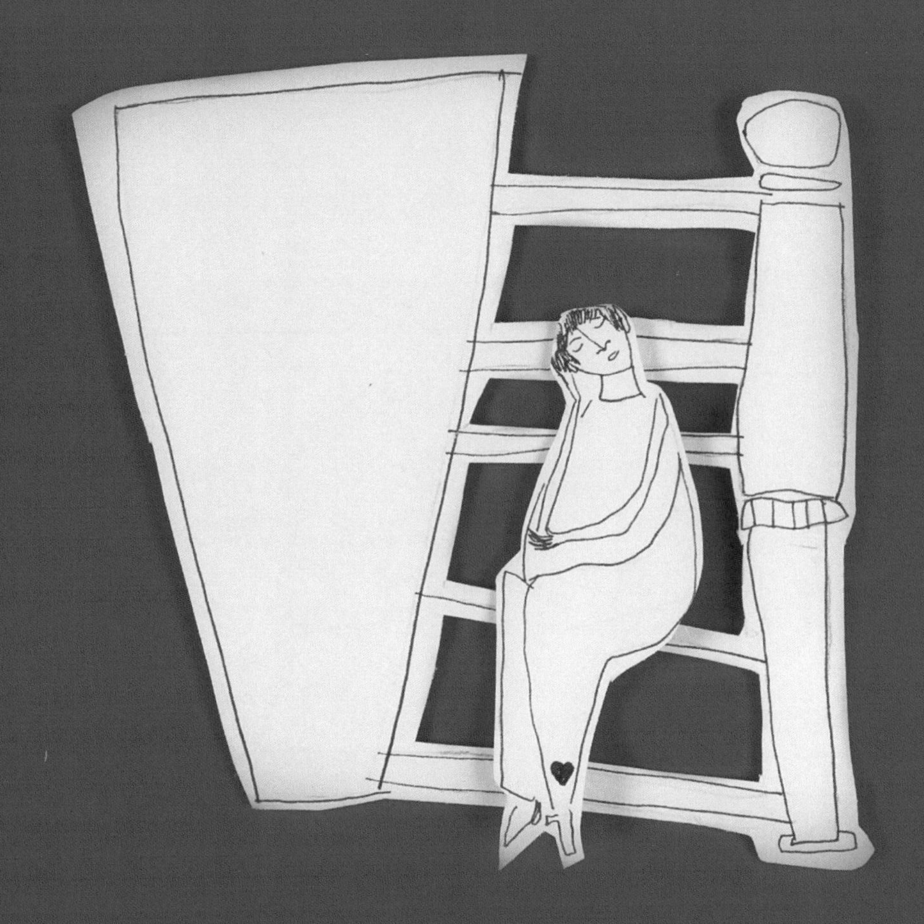

On Kyle's 10th birthday, Kyle's mother invited the whole class to his birthday party.

"Everybody loves dancing. It will be great," she said.

Kyle's stomach tightened.

At school, he heard the kids talking about his party,

"Are you going to that loser's party?"

"No way!" They laughed.

Kyle didn't want to tell his parents what the kids said about him.

The day of the party, Kyle's relatives came to help blow up balloons and make dinner. Kyle's mother dimmed the lights in the basement.

"We're all set. Everything looks great." Kyle's mother said with a smile.

Kyle smiled back, but his stomach was in knots.

Kyle played video games with his cousin while they waited for kids to arrive. After an hour, Kyle couldn't pretend that anyone was coming. Even his three oldest friends from kindergarten didn't show up.

"Can we have the cake tomorrow night. I don't feel so well," Kyle said. His eyes hurt from holding back his tears.

"You bet!" Kyle's mom said with a small smile. Kyle could tell that her eyes hurt too.

That night, after his parents tucked him in, Kyle lay awake in his bed and listened to the owl outside his window. He watched the stars and the moon and wished he could live up there. Kyle knew he had to talk to his parents, but he was afraid they would hate him, like the kids in his class, if they knew the truth about him. Kyle felt alone in the world.

On Monday morning, Kyle wouldn't get out of bed. He hurt all over.

"Kyle, I know you're upset about the party," his mother said. "I know it's been hard with some of the boys in class, but don't let them ruin it for you."

Kyle just moaned.

"Sticks and stones can break your bones, but names can never harm you," Kyle's father said. "Let's go. You have to go to school."

Kyle pulled the covers over his head, "I'm not going. I can't go. It's not going to work out. It will never work out for me. I'm a mistake!" Kyle screamed. "I only look like a boy, but I'm not like other boys," Kyle cried.

"What are you saying?" Kyle's mother asked.

"I can't live like this anymore. I don't belong here. Everyone hates me. I want to live in heaven." Kyle cried from under the covers.

"Is it because you feel like a girl?" Kyle's mother asked as she pulled down his covers. Everything stopped. Kyle's room was still. It felt like all the air was gone. Kyle lifted up the covers and his parents scooped him up into their arms and hugged him for a long time.

“It’s okay. We’ll figure this out,” Kyle’s mother said.

“You don’t hate me?” Kyle asked.

“We’ll always love you. Nothing could ever change that,” Kyle’s parents said.

At first, Kyle's parents were confused. They didn't know what to do, but the more Kyle shared his feelings, the better things got.

It took time and help from lots of people, but Kyle's parents understood that Kyle couldn't live as a boy anymore… Kyle had to live as Kayla.

Over the next few months, Kayla's family and friends dropped off dresses, skirts, and shoes for her. Kayla's mom took her to get a new hairstyle and manicure at the beauty salon. Kayla couldn't stop looking in the mirror and smiling!

“Let’s go Kayla, they’ll be here any minute,” Kayla’s mom called upstairs.

Kayla got up from her bed, took a deep breath and pulled up her skirt.

I can do this! She thought.

Kayla’s heart jumped when the doorbell rang. She wasn’t sure what her oldest friends would think of her as a girl.

Kayla stood at the top of the stairs as her mother opened the door.

Kayla’s knees shook as she looked down at her friends holding a birthday cake.

In less than a second, her three friends ran up to Kayla, put down the cake, and wrapped their arms around her.

Kayla felt loved.

It wasn't easy at first. Lots of kids and teachers at school didn't understand. Some kids and parents in the community didn't accept Kayla and were mean. They whispered behind her back, but now Kayla's three friends stood by their friend and asked Kayla to sit with them at lunch.

Year

after year

after year…

Kayla has lots of family, friends and teachers that accept her for the girl she is.

Kayla still looks out at the stars at night, but now she feels them sparkle for her.

Kayla thinks, *it's important to love what feels different to you because when you do, your heart grows stronger.*

Author's Note

Many gender diverse kids report being physically bullied or emotionally abused. There is a scarcity of laws protecting transgender or gender non-conforming kids in school. This book needs to be shared for the many children and their families who may feel like Kayla, who fit into the increasingly valued voices of those who have not been heard. This story is for them. They need to know that their story is being told. And in this moment in time, people are starting to listen.

The profits from the sale of the book will go to Trans Youth Family Allies.

Please visitwww.whenkaylawaskyle.com for more information.

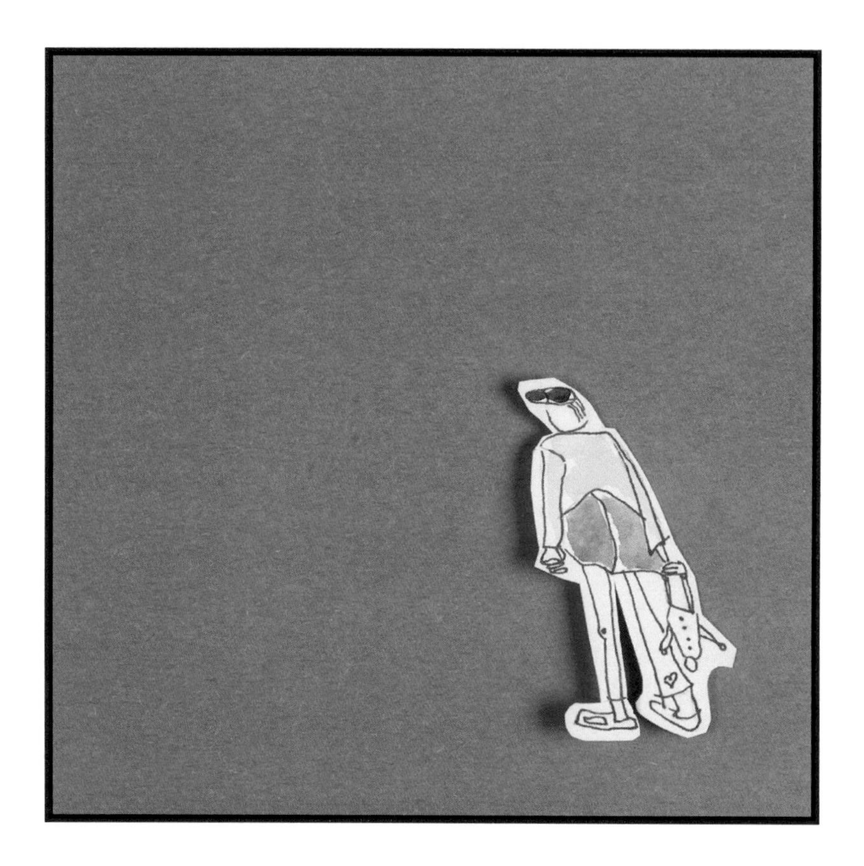

Resources:

PFLAG: Parents, Family, Friends of Lesbian and Gay
TNET: PFLAG'S Transgender network: While PFLAG provides support, education, and advocacy for the whole LGBT community, PFLAG's Transgender Network – or TNET – specifically focuses on support for transgender people and their parents, families, and friends. It provides education on some issues unique to the transgender community.
www.pflag.org

Trans Youth Family Allies: TYFA, empowers children and families
by partnering with educators, service providers and communities to develop supportive environments in which gender may be expressed and respected.
1-888-462-8932
www.imatyfa.org

GLESN: The Gay, Lesbian & Straight Education Network strives to assure that each member of every school community is valued and respected regardless of sexual orientation or gender identity/ expression.
www.glesn.org

CPSIA information can be obtained at www.ICGtesting.com
Printed in the USA
BVIW12n2124100917
494510BV00002B/3